The Perfect,
Man Handbook

Paul M. Onischuk

authorHOUSE®

AuthorHouse™
1663 Liberty Drive
Bloomington, IN 47403
www.authorhouse.com
Phone: 1-800-839-8640

First published by AuthorHouse 5/10/2011

ISBN: 978-1-4567-3331-5 (sc)
ISBN: 978-1-4567-3332-2 (e)

Library of Congress Control Number: 2011901887

Printed in the United States of America

For Mom and Dad, who taught by example.

CONTENTS

PROLOGUE

There is no such thing as a perfect man; but this fact should not dissuade efforts to define and emulate such person with the intent of improving some aspects of those destined to fall short. Take a moment, close your eyes, and briefly think about what a "perfect man" may think, act, and look like. What did you come up with? Although your list is surely diverse and unique to your perspective, I believe you will be hard-pressed to find fault with a man that is kind, confident, strong, ambitious (not to acquire or achieve more personally but for the benefit of others), and accommodating. So, for the sake of argument (and the fact that I am unable to see your list), let's use these characteristics as a baseline; map them to what all men are comprised of, namely, their disposition, their relationships, and their presence; and see what happens.

I'm sure in your experience you became aware of men that have made significant adjustments in their lives, though, perhaps, in an inopportune or protracted manner. Take, for example, the following:

- Someone who quits smoking/begins eating right/ starts an exercise regimen after experiencing a health setback;

- Someone who, in the wrenches of divorce, reacts by displaying newfound attention and love toward their previously neglected children;

- Someone who, confronted with their own mortality, decides to finally make "peace" with previously scorned family members;

- Someone who, facing a significantly damaged relationship, decides to initiate key conversations that should have occurred some time ago; and

- Someone who, now fully comfortable with their financial situation, decides to take on a charitable cause.

Although I am relatively young (39 as of this writing), trust me when I say that life is short, and certain decisions need to be made early before it's too late. Why wait to forgive someone who wronged you? Why defer proper eating and exercising routines that will provide the physique you always wanted? Why delay professional and career decisions that will increase time with your family and truly improve the quality of your life? There are no justifiable answers to these and the multitude of similar questions that have potential to significantly impact your life and must be faced to address your ultimate constraint: time. Time is a limited resource that no one is immune from. What will you do with your time and how will you manage the time you have left?

From a micro perspective, I hope that you spend some of your time reading, considering, and meditating on the contents of this book. Although I do not profess to have all the answers (as no one should), I guarantee that the following considerations, even when approached individually and non-sequentially, will have a material impact on your life and those that you come in contact with.

With regard to approaching the following contents individually and non-sequentially, this book has been structured according to men's disposition, men's relationships (with everyone, significant other, friends, work, and money), and men's presence—key components of men's lives that are further expanded upon according to the aforementioned characteristics of kind, confident, strong, ambitious, and accommodating. So, if you need to work on your relationship with your significant other (who doesn't) and desire to be more kind, you may direct your attention to that section exclusively. If you wish to be more kind in general, you may reference this characteristic under each component of men's lives, or simply thumb through the headers on the upper right hand corner of each page to look for re-occurrences of this characteristic that begin in bold under each component. A key takeaway here is that this book need not be approached in its entirety or sequentially, so use it as your situation and needs dictate.

With regard to those you come in contact with, it is critically important that we include women in this process as well. Quite simply, it is just as important that women read this book as it is for men to. Although the focus of this book is specific to men, sufficient benefits will be afforded women as an increased understanding of what they should reasonably and idealistically expect from men will provide effective opportunities for selection and coaching. By either avoiding or coaching a sub-par spouse, companion, friend, or business associate, women will require and affect improvement in men; thereby, resulting in a better end result. However, if women settle for men that fail to meet their needs or treat them in a way that they do not prefer to be treated, they enable undesirable behaviors and inhibit such improvement.

We, both men and women, need more "perfect" men in our lives. The aforementioned characteristics of a "perfect man," however, are not exclusive to men only. For example, if men are strong, it does not imply that women need to be weak. Men and women may both be strong, but men need to differentiate themselves by the degree and the way in which they convey their strength. By doing so, it provides the opportunity for both men and women to own these characteristics, while allowing for necessary differentiation, which serves the important role of attracting and complementing men and women in the first place. Men may also emulate these characteristics without changing their roles, responsibilities, or expectations (particularly those held by women). By simply increasing their awareness of these characteristics and letting them guide their actions, men will be able to impact how they are perceived and affect desired change in their lives.

Although I hope you will agree that the following information is presented in a logical, easily understandable, and readily referenced manner, I acknowledge that the endeavor of defining a "perfect man" is a bit of a challenge. There are surely considerations and characteristics I may have missed, and emerging items that may come to the forefront given constant change in men's expectations and responsibilities. Although I compiled the following to be as complete as possible, please use the Notes pages to add other considerations you may discover. Also, remember that there is no such thing as perfection, but that should not keep us from trying.

DISPOSITION

Your actions flow from your disposition (your values, your foundation, and your filter), and your disposition has potential to affect all areas of your life. To effectively direct your actions, you must begin with your disposition. Without a solid understanding and adoption of the following, efforts to establish healthy relationships and exude an appropriate presence will fail.

1. Believe that good exists
   in all people and things.

2. Act as though all men and women are created equal.

3. Understand that everyone
is someone's child.

4. Be thankful.

5. Refrain from controlling others. Rather, allow others to act independently and freely, empowered to make their own decisions.

6. Be lighthearted and patient.

7. Practice random acts of kindness, particularly when no one is watching.

8. Respect the Earth.

9. Know that all good
things are plentiful.

10.   Understand that your
thoughts and actions, no
matter how small, are real
and reverberate in time.

11.   Think before you act.

12. Understand that there is a time for everything.

13. Appreciate the variety of life, including its ups and downs.

14.   Believe that within every challenge is opportunity.

15.   Know that you
      are imperfect.

16. Refrain from defining your self-concept by comparing yourself to others.

17.   Find and practice religion.

18.   Remain true to your beliefs and speak up about things that matter, even when they are contrary to popular opinion.

19.   Understand the
power of perspective.

20.   Acknowledge that you
do not know everything…

…and listen, especially
when you do not know.

21.   Do for yourself, if
you are able…

…but reach out for
help when in need.

22.   Remove yourself from controversial or dangerous situations, particularly those that may result in harm to you or others.

23. Let go of the unrealistic expectation of true happiness.

24. Understand that material possessions do not provide lasting happiness.

25.   Align your goals
to your values.

26. Take calculated risks.

Disposition
Ambitious

27. Try new things.

28.   Seek out activities
where you derive both
pleasure and meaning.

29.   Let go of the unrealistic expectation of unconditional love, but attempt to love unconditionally (e.g. without expecting anything in return).

30. Know that it is better to give than it is to receive.

31. Simplify.

RELATIONSHIPS
Everyone

Your relationships define who you are. If you wish to affect who you are and how you are perceived, manage your relationships.

32.   Place others' deserving needs above your own.

33. Forgive others.

34. Greet others, then follow-up
with an honest compliment.

35. Say please and
thank you often.

36. Convey your expectations
of a relationship, no
matter how casual.

37. Help someone in
need privately.

38.   Be good in bad times.

39.   Refrain from emulating an inappropriate response received from others…

…and allow a reasonable "cool down" period before responding when angered.

40.   Be on-time, which is
an indication of respect.

41.   Compliment publicly...

...and confront privately,
but only when necessary.

42. Agree to disagree
when appropriate.

43.   Refrain from saying
adverse things about others,
especially when they are
not in your presence.

44. Do not share information
obtained in confidence.

45.   Conduct yourself
on the Internet as you
would in person.

46.   Admit fault when and
where appropriate.

47. Remain steadfast
to your values.

48.   Determine who
you can trust.

49.   Give others a voice
to understand their
point-of-view first.

50.   Practice active listening.

51.   React after gathering
sufficient information.

52.   Shoot for win-win,
mutually beneficial solutions.

53.   Anticipate others' needs and deliver without prompting.

54. Keep promises.

55.   Offer advice, if asked.

56. Use a person's preferred name, as conveyed in written correspondence or obtained from conversations with them.

57.　Respect others' personal space.

58.   Let others go first.

59.   Ask if it is a good time to talk upon reaching someone by telephone, as they may not be unoccupied the moment you called.

60. Give individuals your undivided attention, understanding that anyone in your presence takes precedence over the telephone, mobile phone, computer, or television.

61.   Refrain from monopolizing conversations; thereby, allowing others to contribute equally.

RELATIONSHIPS
Significant Other

62. Share your thoughts
and feelings.

63.   Distribute wealth equitably,
particularly in a relationship
with disparate earnings.

64.   Consult your significant other before making expensive purchases—unless it is a gift for them.

65. Arrange for flowers
periodically, particularly
when not expected.

66. Clean up after yourself
(i.e., put things away after
taking them out).

67. Acknowledge other women, but never stare.

68.   Refrain from leaving a "to do list" when you are away.

69.   Never criticize your significant other's cooking.

70.   Clean up and do the dishes when your significant other cooks.

71.   Close the door when using the bathroom.

72. Know that relationships
(especially marital) are
not disposable and require
continued maintenance,
repair, and renewal.

73.   Discuss concerns in your relationship before resorting to deceit or unfaithfulness.

74.   Never remove your wedding ring and avoid situations where you may consider doing so.

75.   Renew your vows.

76.   Never express yourself physically when angered.

77.   Understand that children
are our future and your
children are your legacy.

78.   Set mutually agreeable
expectations regarding
money and sex, but strive
for a reasonable degree of
spontaneity in both respects.

79.   Ensure a reasonable balance between household, children, significant other, and personal responsibilities.

80. Respect the challenges
of child raising, contribute
equally, and solicit
assistance when needed.

81.   Understand that free time
is shared time, particularly
if you are a parent.

82.   Arrange "free days" for your significant other, especially when she is the primary caregiver of your children.

83.   Fuel, maintain, and clean your significant other's car or, alternatively, arrange for someone else to do so.

84.   Pay child/spousal support, if divorced.

85.   Sleep on the side of the bed closest to the bedroom door. Wake up to investigate any "bumps-in-the-night," while insisting that your significant other remains in bed.

86. Accommodate servicemen appointments and significant deliveries.

87.   Place your significant other's
and your order after gathering
their preference for the meal.

88.   Accompany your significant other at social events.

89.   Walk on the curb/street
side when accompanying
your significant other.

90.   Every night, kiss your
significant other and tell
them that you love them.

RELATIONSHIPS
Friends

91.   Share information, but be cautious of divulging personal information or being critical of your significant other during discussions with friends.

92.   Keep friendships platonic
and balanced in regard
to other, more significant
relationships (i.e., that with
your significant other).

93.   Choose friends
that you admire.

94. Earn at least three
good friends.

95.   Make time for friends.

[Refer to "Relationships with Everyone" again.]

RELATIONSHIPS
Work

96.   Refrain from bringing
problems at work home and
from bringing problems
at home to work.

97.   Refrain from:

- Using e-mails to replace telephone conversations.

- Drafting long, drawn-out e-mails.

- Omitting salutations and closing remarks in e-mail messages.

- Using all caps in letters and e-mails as it is considered shouting.

98.   Introduce yourself to
new people in the office.

99.   Dress slightly above minimum dress code requirements.

100. Refrain from:

- Placing your hands in your pockets.

- Slouching or resting your head on your hand at meetings.

- Walking hallways slowly or un-purposefully.

- Volunteering information in a difficult situation.

101. Find a good, supportive advisor.

102. Understand that retirement is not an objective in life.

103. Set measurable and attainable goals for yourself and your department and be prepared to discuss actions taken to achieve them without notice.

104. Have your "elevator
speech" ready at all times.

105. When faced with significant career decisions, choose those that allow more time with your family (even at a lesser wage).

106. Manage time by deciding what not to do.

107. Return calls and respond
to e-mails timely.

RELATIONSHIPS
Money

108. Live within your means.

109. Keep expenses from rising to meet income.

110. Know that credit cards are
a necessary evil—necessary to
establish your credit rating and
evil as they enable you to easily
spend beyond your means.

111. Pay off credit card balances each month (i.e., do not purchase items with your credit card that you will not be able to pay for when your statement arrives).

112. Consider a pre-owned car, particularly when available from the original owner or from a dealer, when certified.

PRESENCE

Your presence (i.e., how you are perceived by others) represents who you are to others and is an element of your reality. To influence your reality, manage how you are perceived.

113. Never use offensive
remarks or profanity.

114. Do not interrupt others.

115. Refrain from yawning, itching, belching, spitting, adjusting yourself, passing gas or blowing your nose when around others.

116. Accommodate the aforementioned by excusing yourself to use the restroom.

117. Set your mobile phone to vibrate and excuse yourself if it is necessary to answer it.

118. Avoid noises that may
be annoying to others.

119. Sneeze and cough in the
inset of your arm or use
a cupped hand, but wash
your hands afterwards.

120. Refrain from:

- Eating in the company of others who are not.

- Eating quickly or excessively.

- Slurping or "chugging" beverages (if necessary to drink from a bottle, ensure the beverage pours smoothly).

- Eating off of anyone else's plate.

- Chewing with your mouth open.

121. Never raise your voice
to get your point across.

122. Understand that you
share the air with those
around you; as an abundance
of caution, breathe in and
out through your nose,
particularly in close quarters.

123. Refer to unknown individuals as "Sir" or "Ms." (if you are sure of their gender). Otherwise, say "Pardon me..." or "Excuse me..."

124. Maintain and monitor your posture.

125. Age appropriately.

126. Improve your ability to speak in public by participating in a Toastmasters International (public speaking) club.

127. Keep your mouth closed,
unless you are speaking.

128. Opt for:

- An undershirt.

- A belt.

- Boxer-briefs or boxers.

- Age appropriate clothing.

- Shoe shines.

- Socks that match your pants.

- Hair cuts from a licensed barber, avoiding destination salons or those that are frequented by women.

- Short trimmed or shaved hair, particularly if balding.

- A "clean-cut" look or an appropriate amount of facial hair

129. Shop for your own clothes, preferably alone, but be gracious when others purchase clothes for you.

130. Select your attire when
going out, consulting others
only when needed.

131. Purchase a new suit for
a particularly significant
event and have your suits
professionally tailored.

132. Relax, practice
diaphragmatic breathing.

133. Take dance lessons.

134. Escort your partner to dance; thereby, avoiding her dragging you to do so.

135. Ensure your dance moves are tasteful and appropriate for your age (i.e., avoiding those that jeopardize the safety of those in the surrounding area, involve excessive hip movement, or are considered out-of-date).

136. Drive a comfortable speed above the speed limit. Otherwise, obey the rules of the road.

137. Be fit.

138. Visit your doctor, dentist, optometrist, etc. as needed, but at least once a year.

139. Do not smoke, drink
excessively, or consume
light or diet anything.

140. Shake hands firmly while establishing eye contact; avoiding the "death grip" or "wet noodle."

141. Vacate if your significant
other hosts a gathering of
her friends (a/k/a "girls'
night in") and...

...avoid calling your significant
other on guys' night out
(at least in public).

142. Refrain from:

- Joining your significant other when they are shopping for clothes, shoes, accessories, make-up, etc. or receiving professional services (e.g. haircuts, manicures, waxing/threading, etc.).

- Pampering your self publically.

- Holding your significant other's purse.

- Storing feminine products in your car.

- Having more grooming products/ toiletries than your significant other.

143. Earn a scar.

144. Get a tasteful tattoo that remains, at a minimum, concealed when casually dressed (unless your occupation is a rock star, professional basketball/ football player, or pirate).

145. Avoid:

- Upturned collars (unless employed as a model and the photographer or stylist requests so).

- Rings (other than wedding), bracelets, and earrings (unless employed as a rock star, professional basketball/football player, or pirate).

- Scarves, unless dictated by the weather.

- Speedos (unless employed as an Olympic swimmer or diver).

- Man purses or "fanny packs."

- Dated, worn, or stained clothes.

Avoid (continued):

- Bright, pastel, pink, baby blue, and purple clothes or white pants (unless employed as a painter).

- Sweat pants, unless worn at the gym or involved in a similar physical activity.

- Neck chains.

146. Bathe/shower daily; brush, floss, and rinse with mouthwash twice daily; groom yourself (e.g., cut nails, trim hair, etc.) periodically; and accommodate the aforementioned privately.

147. Wear a wristwatch.

148. Carry an umbrella with any chance of rain and offer to share your umbrella with someone in need.

149. Keep individual, properly
stored tissues on hand.

150. Apply cologne conservatively.

151. Carry a reasonable
amount of cash.

152. Ask someone in your
presence their desire for
_____ before retrieving
_____ for yourself.

153. Have a bottle of champagne
available for significant events.

154. Travel with directions or
a navigation system and stop
for assistance when lost.

155. Offer to drive when
traveling with your
significant other.

156. Offer your seat to a woman, a senior, or, alternatively, anyone in need when traveling by public transportation.

157. Purchase feminine products
only when they are obtained
as part of a larger grocery
or pharmacy purchase.

158. Operate power tools occasionally, but use "human powered" equipment (e.g., push mowers, hand shears, shovels, etc.) as well to incorporate physical activity with household chores.

159. Mow your lawn and shovel your snow, unless a local teen offers lawn or snow shoveling services.

160. Tip according to the quality of service, but at least 10% regardless.

161. Open doors for women.

NOTES